This edition first published in MMXVII by
Book House

Distributed by Black Rabbit Books
P.O. Box 3263
Mankato
Minnesota MN 56002

Cataloging-in-Publication Data is available
from the Library of Congress

Printed in the United States
At Corporate Graphics,
North Mankato, Minnesota

9 8 7 6 5 4 3 2 1

ISBN: 978-1-910706-92-3

EXPLORERS

The Story of
THE RACE TO THE MOON

Jen Green Mark Bergin

BOOK HOUSE

CONTENTS

6 ROCKET POWER
Early dreams of space travel.

8 FIRST IN SPACE
The dawn of the space age.

10 THE RACE BEGINS
The Soviet Union leads in space exploration.

12 AMERICA CATCHES UP
The early years of the Apollo program.

14 DESTINATION: MOON
The Apollo 11 spacecraft.

16 WE HAVE LIFT-OFF!
The launch of Apollo 11.

18 ON COURSE
Apollo 11 leaves Earth's orbit.

20 TOUCHDOWN
Apollo 11 lands on the Moon.

22 ONE GIANT LEAP
Human beings walk on the Moon.

24 MISSION ACCOMPLISHED
Apollo 11 returns safely to Earth.

26 THE END OF APOLLO
The final years of the Moon missions.

28 WHAT HAPPENED NEXT?
Events after the Apollo program.

30 GLOSSARY

32 INDEX

INTRODUCTION

O ne morning in the late 20th century, a tiny silver spacecraft dropped from a black, star-filled sky toward the rocky surface of a minor planet. The craft drifted down slowly, and landed with a puff of dust. It rocked on its landing legs, then steadied. The craft and its occupants were alone in a vast, silent landscape pitted with deep-shadowed craters which stretched away in every direction.

A small hatch opened in the spacecraft. A figure dressed in a bulky suit climbed down the spaceship's ladder and stepped onto the gray, powdery surface. The date was July 21, 1969, and human beings had landed on the Moon. It was just twelve years since the first object made by humans had reached space, and a race to land on the Moon had begun. This brief period had seen enormous advances in science and technology— advances that paved the way for that historic landing on the Moon.

Note: Where the Soviet Union is mentioned throughout the text, this refers to the former USSR.

ROCKET POWER

Hundreds of years before astronauts set foot on the Moon, people had already dreamed of traveling through space. The 16th century author, Francis Godwin, wrote about a trip to the Moon. And Jules Verne's 1865 prophetic tale of man's journey to the Moon inspired later scientists such as Wernher von Braun.

The First Rockets

The first rockets were invented in China about 2,000 years ago.

An American scientist, Robert Goddard, built the first high-altitude rocket in 1926. Goddard's rocket was fueled by gasoline and liquid oxygen, which created hot gases that blasted down to thrust the rocket into the air. It rose 40 feet (12 meters) before falling back to earth.

Rocket Power

By the early 20th century a Russian inventor, Konstantin Tsiolkovsky, thought of using rockets to reach space. In 1903 he suggested that liquid fuel should be used to power rockets, since it could be controlled more easily than solid fuel.

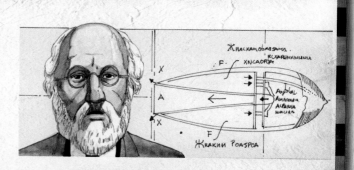

DREAMS OF SPACE TRAVEL

Goddard's Rocket

Like Tsiolkovsky, Goddard realized that only a rocket, which could carry all its own fuel, could escape Earth's gravity to reach space.

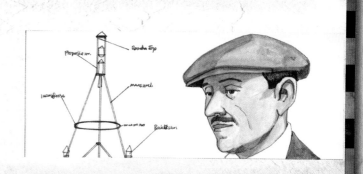

During World War II Germany launched V-2 rockets carrying explosives. Over 1,400 rockets were fired at London. Following Tsiolkovsky's theory, they burned liquid fuel. When Germany was defeated in 1945, von Braun surrendered to the United States army and became an American citizen.

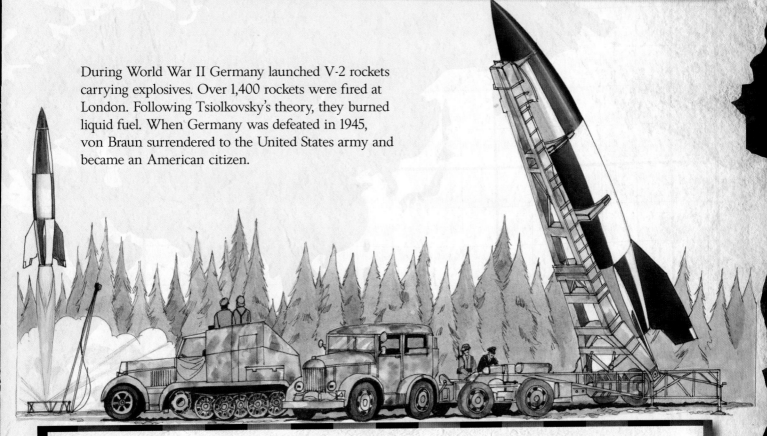

The V-2 Rocket

During World War II Wernher von Braun developed a rocket-powered missile in Germany called the V-2. After the war, von Braun lived in America where he went on to mastermind the American space program, including the Apollo launches.

FIRST IN SPACE

A period of hostility between the Soviet Union and the United States began after World War II. This was known as the Cold War. Both countries wanted to prove that their scientists were making great technological advances. Americans believed that their technology was superior, until the Soviets shot a satellite, Sputnik 1, into space in 1957.

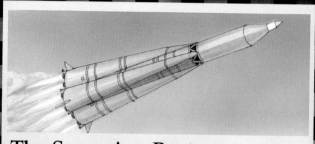

The Space Age Begins
The Soviet space program was led by a brilliant scientist, Sergei Korolyev. By 1957 Soviets had built a powerful rocket, the SS-6. On October 4 the rocket was used to place a satellite, Sputnik 1, in orbit round the Earth.

The first manufactured satellite, Sputnik 1, was a small metal sphere containing a radio transmitter. Long aerials were attached to the sphere. Sputnik ("Traveler") orbited the Earth for 92 days before burning up.

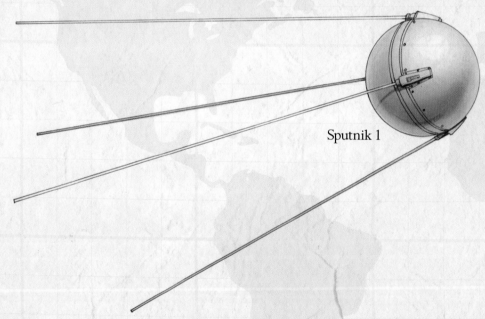

Sputnik 1

Laika
In November 1957 the Soviets followed this success with another impressive first. A second, larger satellite, Sputnik 2, carried a dog called Laika into space. Unfortunately Laika did not survive her trip.

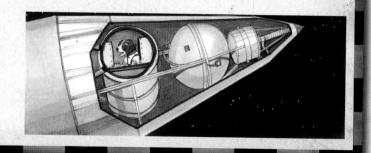

THE DAWN OF THE SPACE AGE

First Man In Space

On April 12, 1961, after more test flights with dogs, the Soviets put the first man in space. Major Yuri Gagarin was the first "cosmonaut"—the Russian word for astronaut. He made a single orbit of the Earth.

A new powerful Soviet rocket was used to launch Gagarin into space. His spacecraft Vostok ("East") 1, was a round capsule on top of an instrument section with rockets which fired to control the craft's position.

A Safe Return

Vostok's capsule glowed with heat as it entered the atmosphere. Gagarin experienced powerful forces called g-forces as his craft slowed down. The cosmonaut parachuted safely down near the River Volga in Russia.

THE RACE BEGINS

Gagarin's success embarrassed the United States. America's National Aeronautics and Space Administration (NASA) had been formed in 1958: its aim was to put a man in space. By 1961 NASA had sent a chimpanzee named Ham on a brief space flight, but while von Braun was perfecting the American rocket, news came of Gagarin's success. In May 1961 the new president, John F Kennedy, vowed that America would place a man on the Moon and return him safely to Earth before 1970. The race was on.

Following the President's speech in 1961, the Moon landing project, codenamed Apollo, was given massive funding.

Americans in space
In 1961 the first American astronaut, Alan Shepard, entered space. In 1962 John Glenn was the first American to orbit the Earth, completing three circuits before splashing down in the Atlantic.

Telstar, the US satellite launched in 1962.

The First Woman In Space
In 1963 the Soviets pressed forward again; Valentina Tereshkova became the first woman in space. She spent almost three days in space, completing 48 orbits.

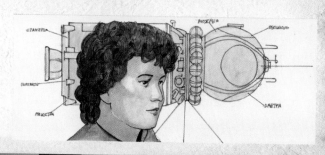

SOVIETS LEAD SPACE EXPLORATION

Voshkod 1

In 1964 the Soviets launched Voshkod 1 ("Sunrise"), carrying three cosmonauts in a cabin filled with air, so there was no need for spacesuits.

In June 1965, American astronaut Edward White walked in space, maneuvering with gas jets from a hand-held gun.

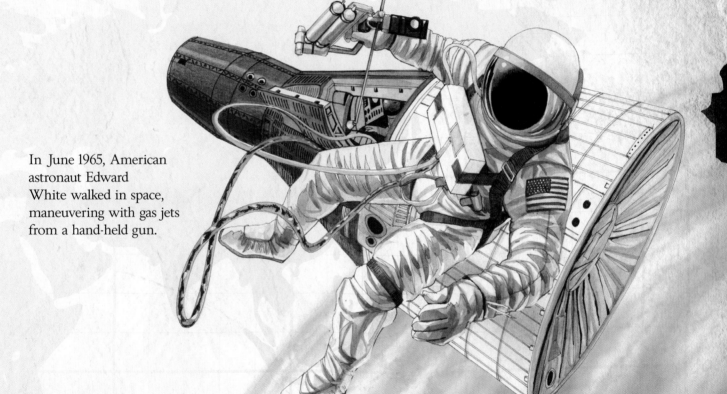

Space Walks

In 1965 Russian cosmonaut Alexei Leonov took the first "walk" in space, putting the Soviets ahead again. The trip was not trouble-free: Leonov struggled to re-enter his craft because his spacesuit made it difficult for him to bend enough to fit back through the hatch.

On re-entry his craft landed off course. The crew spent a night surrounded by wolves before rescue came!

AMERICA CATCHES UP

So, by the early 1960s, America and the Soviet Union were racing one another to the Moon. The Apollo spaceship designed by the Americans consisted of two craft which could fly together but also operate separately: a command ship and a Moon lander. The Moon lander would visit the Moon and then rejoin the main ship for the trip back to Earth. A new rocket would be needed to carry the craft into space. But there were questions about the Moon itself. Was the surface suitable for landing, or was it covered with a layer of dust which a spacecraft would sink into? Both countries sent unmanned craft, called probes, to investigate.

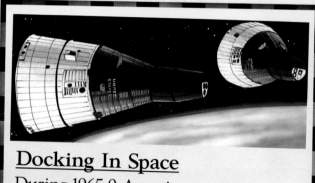

Docking In Space
During 1965-9 American astronauts practiced for the Moon mission in Gemini craft. Two Apollo craft would need to meet and dock (join) in space. In 1965 Geminis 5 and 6 flew within meters of each other.

American probe, Surveyor 3.

THE EARLY YEARS OF APOLLO

The Dark Side Of The Moon

In December 1968 Apollo 8 lifted off. On board, Frank Borman, Jim Lovell, and Bill Anders were the first men to leave Earth's orbit and start traveling to the Moon. On Christmas Eve they became the first astronauts to see the far side of the Moon. The crew spent 20 hours orbiting the Moon before returning safely to Earth.

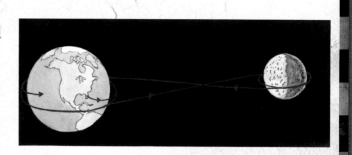

On the Moon's far side, the crew of Apollo 8 lost contact with NASA when the bulk of the Moon blocked out radio signals. Everyone at Mission Control center in Houston, Texas, waited anxiously for the ship to clear the far side and re-establish contact. The mission went without a hitch and returned safely.

Distant World

The Moon is 238,855 miles (384,400 kilometers) from Earth. It took Apollo 8 three days to reach it, traveling at a top speed of 23,860 miles per hour (38,400 km/h).

DESTINATION: MOON

The Apollo 10 mission was planned to test the lunar module in orbit round the Moon. Only if it was completely successful would the landing go ahead. In May 1969, Apollo 10 lifted off and headed for the Moon.

As part of the test-flight, two astronauts in Apollo 10's lunar module descended to within 8.6 miles (14 km) of the Moon's surface, but did not land. They rejoined the main ship and returned to Earth.

The early Apollos
The first six Apollo missions were designed to test von Braun's new Saturn rocket and were unmanned. In March 1969, Apollo 9 astronauts practiced docking the command ship with the lunar module in Earth's orbit.

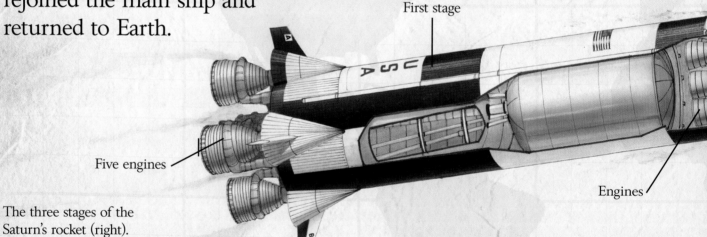

First stage

Five engines

Engines

The three stages of the Saturn's rocket (right).

Apollo 11

In 1969 Apollo 11 was named as the craft scheduled to make the Moon landing. It consisted of three parts, or modules. The command module was nicknamed Columbia and would carry the astronauts for most of the journey and return with them to Earth. Attached to Columbia was the service module which housed the rockets and fuel that would be needed for the round trip to the Moon. The lunar module (Eagle) would take two of the astronauts down to the Moon. After they had explored the surface, the Eagle's rockets would fire to carry them back to Columbia, orbiting above.

THE APOLLO 11 SPACECRAFT

Saturn 5

The Apollo craft was so heavy that von Braun had to design the largest rocket ever built, Saturn 5, to blast it into space. It stood 364 feet (111 meters) tall, and was assembled at Cape Canaveral, Florida, in a building so tall that clouds sometimes gathered at the top at night. The rocket burned a mixture of kerosene and liquid oxygen.

Mission badge

The astronauts picked for the Apollo 11 flight were Neil Armstrong, Edwin "Buzz" Aldrin, and Michael Collins. All three were born in 1930 and were experienced pilots.

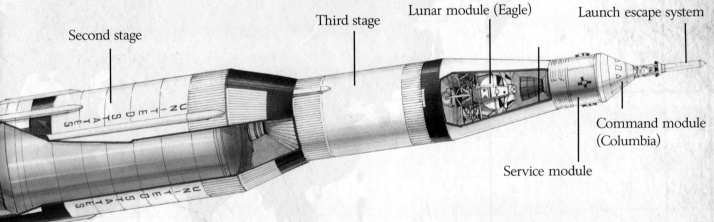

Second stage

Third stage

Lunar module (Eagle)

Launch escape system

Command module (Columbia)

Service module

The Saturn 5 rocket had three stages. Each was jettisoned (cast away) once its fuel was used up. This lightened the load to be carried upward.

In Training

Before the mission, the three astronauts practiced every move in machines called simulators, which worked just like the Apollo craft. Once clear of Earth's gravity, all astronauts experience weightless conditions. Aldrin, Armstrong, and Collins trained underwater to prepare for this.

WE HAVE LIFT-OFF!

Launch Day for Apollo 11's mission was July 16, 1969. The morning was clear and bright as the astronauts were driven across the base to the launch pad where the Saturn 5 rocket towered high above it. The astronauts were taken to the top in the launch tower lift. Two hours before take-off the three astronauts took their seats in the command module. Buzz Aldrin, who would help fly the lunar module, sat in the center. On Aldrin's left was Neil Armstrong, the flight commander. He would be the first to step on the Moon. On his right sat Michael Collins, the command module pilot, who would stay on board. At 9.32 am Apollo 11 was cleared for take-off.

On the Launch Pad

Dressed in bulky spacesuits, the astronauts were helped into their seats aboard Columbia. Then Columbia's hatch was closed. Mission Control informed the astronauts: "You are go for launch."

Mission control in Houston, Texas.

Spectators

Thousands of spectators had gathered at a safe distance to see Apollo 11 blast off. Millions more followed the event on television or radio, as the astronauts made their final preparations for take-off.

THE LAUNCH OF APOLLO 11

Lift-off

"Three, two, one, zero...we have lift-off!" – the excited ground crew at Cape Canaveral watched as Apollo 11 rose into the air. The engines of the Saturn 5 rocket burned 16.5 tons of fuel per second and produced one of the loudest sounds ever heard.

After three minutes, the launch escape tower which had fitted over the command module was jettisoned. Now the astronauts could see out.

Escape tower jettisoned.

Heading into space

Nine minutes into the flight, the second rocket stage burnt out and was jettisoned. The third stage engines took over as the rocket roared upward. Eleven minutes after take-off, Apollo 11 and the third stage rocket reached Earth's orbit. Final checks were made before heading for the Moon.

ON COURSE

Three hours into Apollo 11's flight, Mission Control in Houston gave the astronauts permission to head for the Moon. The engines of the third stage Saturn rocket blasted the spacecraft free of Earth's orbit. Then, as Apollo hurtled toward the Moon, Michael Collins took the center seat for a difficult maneuver. He had to disengage Columbia from the rocket and turn around to dock with the lunar module, which had been housed inside the third stage. Collins performed this delicate operation perfectly.

On TV

During the flight, a TV camera on board Apollo 11 gave audiences on Earth a tour of the ship and showed the men working in zero gravity.

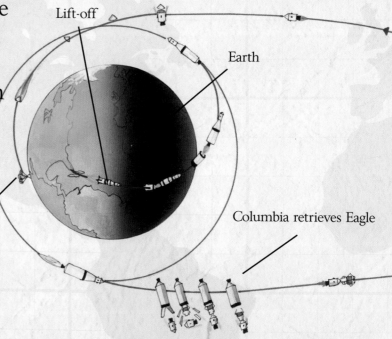

Lift-off

Earth

Columbia retrieves Eagle

Splashdown

Docking

Collins maneuvered the command module of Apollo 11 toward Eagle with the help of the small rocket thrusters on the sides of the service module. Then Columbia docked gently with the lunar module. Collins reversed to disengage it from the Saturn rocket.

Then, with Eagle firmly attached, Apollo 11 headed for the Moon.

Supplies

Apollo was well stocked with supplies. Its emergency survival kit included a life raft in case the crew landed off course on return. To save on weight, food was freeze-dried and sealed in packets. A typical meal was chicken or salmon with rice, pudding, cocoa, and juice.

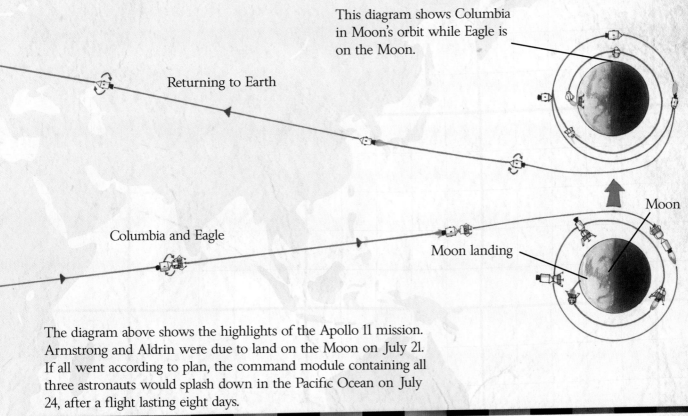

This diagram shows Columbia in Moon's orbit while Eagle is on the Moon.

Returning to Earth

Columbia and Eagle

Moon

Moon landing

The diagram above shows the highlights of the Apollo 11 mission. Armstrong and Aldrin were due to land on the Moon on July 21. If all went according to plan, the command module containing all three astronauts would splash down in the Pacific Ocean on July 24, after a flight lasting eight days.

Time To Rest

During rest periods the astronauts slept in sleeping bags tied below their seats so that they would not float away across the cabin.

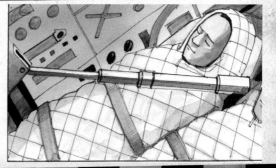

TOUCHDOWN

On July 19, Apollo 11 reached the Moon. The astronauts fired Columbia's rockets to enter the Moon's orbit. On July 20, the astronauts, who had spent most of the trip in overalls, put on their spacesuits. Neil Armstrong and Buzz Aldrin floated through the connecting tunnel into Eagle, leaving Collins alone in Columbia.

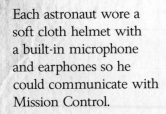

Getting Dressed
The Apollo astronauts wore spacesuits at critical times such as take-off and re-entry. Getting dressed was quite a lengthy process.

Each astronaut wore a soft cloth helmet with a built-in microphone and earphones so he could communicate with Mission Control.

The Eagle Has Wings

The two craft separated as they went behind the Moon again. Columbia continued to orbit the Moon, while Eagle fired its descent engine to slow down for the landing. "The Eagle has wings," Armstrong announced.

APOLLO 11 LANDS ON THE MOON

Danger

As Eagle neared the surface, Armstrong spotted that they were about to land on very rough ground. If the craft tipped over, it would not be able to take off again. The two men would be stranded on the Moon.

During the final moments of descent, Armstrong wrestled with the controls as Aldrin called out the craft's height and speed. Fuel ran out just as one of Eagle's feet touched the dusty ground.

The Eagle Has Landed

Armstrong took control of the landing, slowed Eagle's descent, and steered the craft away from a crater. With seconds to spare it landed safely. There was silence, and then the calm voice of Neil Armstrong said:

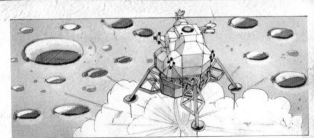

"Houston, Tranquillity Base here. The Eagle has landed."

ONE GIANT LEAP

It had been planned that the astronauts would sleep for four hours before going outside. However, they were too excited to rest.

Armstrong and Aldrin got into their life-support units and protective clothing. Armstrong opened Eagle's hatch, then stepped down onto the Moon.

"That's one small step for a man, one giant leap for mankind," he said. Buzz Aldrin joined him, and the two astronauts planted the American flag. They listened to their radios as Richard Nixon, the new American president, congratulated them on the success of one of the greatest achievements of all time.

Armstrong jumped down onto the Moon.

Left on the Moon
Footprints left on the Moon by Armstrong and Aldrin will last for thousands of years. There is no wind or rain to blow or wash them away.

Walking on the Moon
On the Moon's surface, Armstrong and Aldrin practiced moving around in gravity one-sixth the strength of Earth's. They tried walking, bouncing, and jumping, but found walking worked best.

HUMANS WALK ON THE MOON

Experiments

NASA scientists had given the astronauts a number of tasks to carry out on the Moon. This included taking scientific measurements, setting up an instrument to measure "Moonquakes," and collecting Moon soil. The flag planted by the astronauts was held out straight by a metal rod along the top, because there is no wind to make the flag flutter.

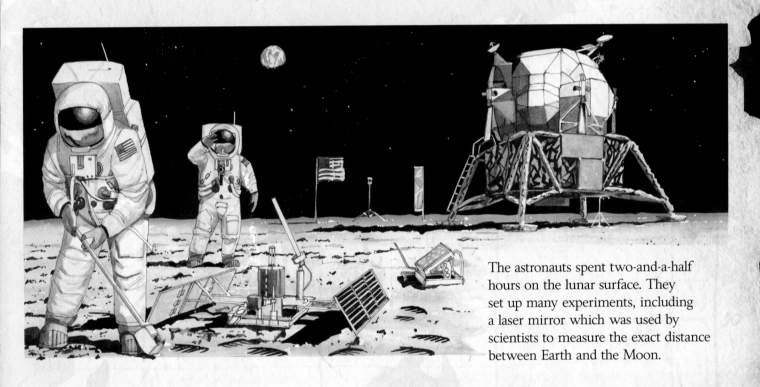

The astronauts spent two-and-a-half hours on the lunar surface. They set up many experiments, including a laser mirror which was used by scientists to measure the exact distance between Earth and the Moon.

For All Mankind

The astronauts also left medals and badges on the Moon in memory of all those who had died during the history of space travel. During the Moon trip Neil Armstrong uncovered a metal plaque to mark the first Moon visit. It reads "We came in peace for all mankind."

MISSION ACCOMPLISHED

Their tasks completed, the astronauts returned to Eagle. Armstrong was the last to leave. He climbed the ladder, squeezed through the hatch, and closed it behind him. Eagle's ascent rocket was the only part of the Apollo 11 spacecraft which had no back-up system. If the rocket failed they would be trapped on the Moon. But it fired smoothly and the little craft blasted upward to meet Columbia, which was orbiting above to take the astronauts home.

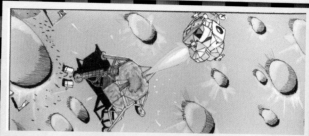

Take-Off from the Moon

Back in the lunar module, the astronauts prepared for take-off. Aldrin anxiously fired Eagle's ascent engine and Eagle took off.

The two craft docked successfully. Then Collins opened the connecting hatch, and Armstrong and Aldrin floated through to join him. Eagle was abandoned as the command module, Columbia, headed back to Earth.

Back on Columbia

Alone in Columbia round the far side of the Moon, Collins was out of contact with Earth and the other astronauts. A newspaper called him "the loneliest man in the universe." He watched eagerly as Eagle approached.

APOLLO 11 RETURNS TO EARTH

Re-entry

Apollo 11 approached the Earth at a speed of 16,700 miles per hour (27,000 km/h). Columbia then separated from the service module. The command module was coated with a special layer to withstand the heat of re-entry to keep the astronauts safe. As Columbia dropped through the air, large parachutes opened to slow its descent.

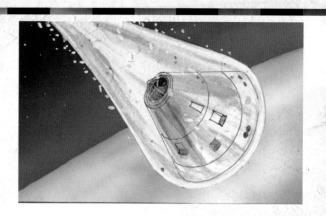

In an isolation container on board the Hornet, the astronauts were greeted by President Nixon.

Back On Earth

Columbia splashed down in the Pacific Ocean. A helicopter from the US navy ship Hornet arrived and the men were winched up and flown back to the ship. There they entered the isolation container for their quarantine.

THE END OF APOLLO

Six more Apollo missions were launched after Apollo 11. Five were successful, but Apollo 13 was nearly a disaster. About 205,000 miles (330,000 km) from Earth, an explosion on board damaged the craft. The crew had to rely on supplies of power, water, and breathable air from their lunar module as they looped around the Moon and headed back to Earth. They splashed down safely. The other five Apollo missions landed on the Moon. Meanwhile, the Soviet Union had concentrated on putting space stations in Earth orbit, and sending probes without cosmonauts to explore space.

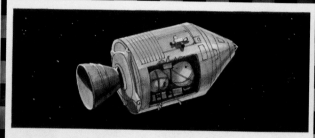

Unlucky 13
Two days into the Apollo 13 mission, an explosion badly damaged the command module's life-support system. The Moon landing was abandoned and the crew only just made it safely back to Earth.

In 1975 a Soviet Soyuz craft docked with an American Apollo in space. The crews visited each other.

Living In Space
Astronauts spending long periods on board space stations must exercise daily or their muscles will weaken. In zero gravity bathing is difficult, because the water tends to float away. Special showers help astronauts to keep clean in space.

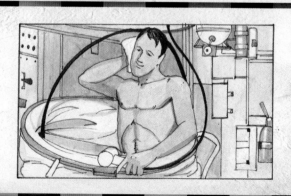

THE FINAL MOON MISSIONS

Buggies

On the later Apollo missions astronauts traveled on the Moon's surface in buggies called lunar roving vehicles. These were battery-powered and carried astronauts up to 3.5 miles (6 km) from the lunar module to explore and carry out experiments.

The End of the Apollo Program

In 1972, Apollo 17 was the last mission with a crew to be sent to the Moon. Astronauts Eugene Cernan and Harrison Schmitt spent 22 hours on the Moon's surface. America then concentrated on building a space station called Skylab. It was launched in 1974 but only operated for six months. By the early 1970s the Soviet Union had gained more experience than the Americans in operating space stations. In 1974 cosmonauts spent a record 63 days in the space station Salyut 4.

The United States spent enormous sums of money on the Apollo project. By the time the Apollo 17 astronauts left the Moon, the project had cost a staggering $25 billion. Each expensive Apollo craft was only used once, then thrown away. In the 1980s and 1990s, both America and the Soviet Union developed reusable spacecraft, built to fly a series of missions, not just one. The Soviet Union has led in the development of space stations, and both countries have sent probes to other planets in our solar system. In recent years other countries, including China, Japan, and Europe, have also begun their own space programs.

The space shuttle is America's reusable spacecraft. It was first launched in 1981. It launches like a rocket, with the aid of strap-on booster rockets and a large main fuel tank, which is jettisoned soon after take-off.

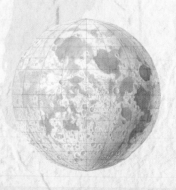

WHAT HAPPENED NEXT?

The shuttle carries new satellites into orbit. It may also carry up to seven astronauts on board. They may leave the craft in spacesuits to repair satellites and other space equipment. Outside the craft, astronauts move around using a Manned Maneuvering Unit (MMU), a pack containing a life-support system and gas jets for moving around.

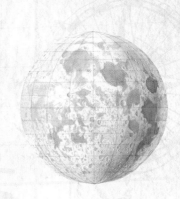

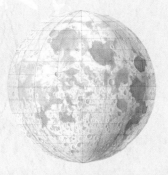

In 1992 American astronauts spent eight hours in space repairing the communications satellite Intelstat 6. When the shuttle's tasks are done, it returns to Earth and lands on a runway, like an airplane. Within two weeks it can be ready for another mission. The shuttle project has been mostly successful, although it had a major setback in 1986. Just after lift-off, the shuttle Challenger caught fire and exploded, killing all seven crew. After this disaster, the project was re-examined carefully to find out what had gone wrong and to make sure it never happened again.

After success with early prototype space stations, the Soviet Union launched space station Mir in 1986. Since then Mir has been occupied continuously by different crews who spend months in space doing research. Soviet cosmonauts have set the records for the longest periods spent in space. Yuri Romanenko spent over a year in space, on three separate missions.

Since the 1970s, probes without crews have revealed many of the secrets of our solar system. The American probe Mariner 2 was first to visit another planet, Venus, in 1962. Mariner 9 orbited Mars. Voyagers 1 and 2 were launched in 1977. They visited Jupiter, Saturn, and Uranus and then left the solar system. They are still sending back signals. The Hubble space telescope was launched in 1990 and repaired by astronauts in 1993. Orbiting high above the Earth, this powerful, giant telescope sends back the clearest pictures yet of distant stars out in deep space.

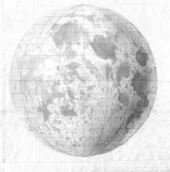

GLOSSARY

Altitude
Height, usually above sea level.

Atmosphere
A layer of gases, including oxygen, surrounding Earth.

Booster
A rocket engine strapped to a spacecraft which gives a short burst of extra power, particularly during take-off.

Cosmonaut
The Russian word for astronaut.

Docking
The linking of two craft in space.

G force
A measure of the force of gravity.

Jettison
To release or throw away.

Liquid fuel
A fuel normally in gas form, but which has been made into liquid through extreme cooling.

Lunar
Relating to the Moon.

Maneuver
A planned movement, or to move.

Module
A section of a spacecraft.

Orbit
The curved path of one object circling another.

Probe
A small craft not built to carry human passengers.

Prototype
An original model.

Simulator
A machine built to imitate the conditions of another environment.

Splashdown
A sea-landing after a space flight.

Stage
A section of a rocket.

Thrust
The pushing power produced by a rocket's engine.

Thruster
A small rocket motor used by a spacecraft to maneuver.

Zero gravity
The condition of weightlessness that exists beyond the pull of gravity.

Quarantine
A period passed in isolation, for health reasons.

Re-entry
The return of a spacecraft to Earth's atmosphere.

Satellite
An object circling a larger body in space, such as a planet. The Moon is a satellite of Earth.

INDEX

A
Aldrin, Edwin, "Buzz" 14,
  15, 16, 19, 21, 22, 23, 24, 25
Apollo space program,
  launch of 10
Apollo 8 13
Apollo 9 14
Apollo 10 14, 15
Apollo 11
  astronaut training 14, 15
  heads for the Moon 18, 19
  launch of 16, 17
  Moon landing 5, 20, 21
  Moon walk 22, 23
  returns to Earth 24, 25
  spacecraft 14, 15
Apollo 13 26
Apollo 17 26, 28
Armstrong, Neil 14, 15, 16,
  19, 20, 21, 22, 23, 24, 25

B
von Braun, Wernher 6, 7, 9,
  14, 15

C
Cold War 8
Collins, Michael 14, 15, 16,
  18, 19, 20, 24, 25

E
Explorer 1 satellite 9

G
Gagarin, Yuri 8, 9
Gemini spacecraft 11, 12, 14
Glenn, John 10
Goddard, Robert 6, 7

H
Hubble telescope 29

K
Kennedy, John F. 10, 20
Korolyev, Sergei 8

L
Leonov, Alexei 11

M
Mercury spacecraft 10, 11
Mir space station 29

N
National Aeronautics and
  Space Administration
  (NASA) 10, 23

Nixon, Richard 22, 25

P
probes 12, 26, 28, 29, 31

S
Salyut 4 space station 27
Saturn 5 rocket 14, 15, 16, 17,
  18, 19
Shepard, Alan 10
Skylab 27
Soyuz spacecraft 10, 26
space shuttle Challenger 29
space shuttles 28, 29
space stations 26, 27, 28
Sputnik satellites 8, 9

T
Tereshkova, Valentina 10
Tsiolkovsky, Konstantin 6, 7

V
Voskhod spacecraft 10, 11
Vostok spacecraft 8, 9, 10
Voyager probes 29

W
White, Edward 11